|| Hanuman Chalisa ||

GRAPEVINE BOOKS

Published by

GRAPEVINE INDIA PUBLISHERS PVT LTD

www.grapevineindia.com
Delhi | Mumbai
email: grapevineindiapublishers@gmail.com

Ordering Information:
Quantity sales: Special discounts are available on quantity purchases by corporations, associations, and others. For details, reach out to the publisher.

First published by Grapevine India 2025

Significance of Hanuman Chalisa

The Hanuman Chalisa stands as an enduring expression of unwavering devotion to Lord Hanuman, renowned for his unbreakable faith and surrender to Lord Rama. Th s sacred hymn, known as the 'Hanuman Chalisa,' was crafted by the revered Saint Goswami Tulsidas, who authored the epic Tulsi Ramayana (Ramacharitamanasa). Tradition holds that Saint Tulsidas, while in poor health, composed the Hanuman Chalisa as a means of seeking divine intervention. Th ough the act of composing and singing praises to Lord Hanuman, Tulsidas experienced a remarkable recovery.

Th s profound composition consists of 40 verses, each brimming with reverent praises for Lord Hanuman. The Hanuman Chalisa is composed in Avadhi, a dialect of the Hindi language spoken in Ayodhya, the sacred birthplace of Lord Rama.

Benefits of Chanting Hanuman Chalisa

As the verses of the Hanuman Chalisa are revealed one by one, they illuminate the multifaceted qualities of Lord Hanuman. Devotees recite and sing this hymn with a deep-seated belief that Hanuman, the supreme devotee of Lord Rama, will bestow his blessings upon them. Th s sacred chant is believed to grant protection from ailments, adversaries, and adversities. Lord Hanuman is revered as the deity of vitality, and worshipping him is thought to augment our life force. An enhanced life force provides us with the inner strength to overcome fear, distrust, and doubt, empowering us to undertake any endeavor with confide ce.

Does Hanuman Chalisa have Astrological Benefits?

Hanuman Chalisa has astrological signifi ance as well. It is found to be deeply successful in controlling the malefic impacts of Saturn's transit or Saturn's major or minor periods. Those under the negative impact of planet will discover incredible help and advantage with the regular recitation of the Chalisa 8 times on a Saturday.

Those with mangal dosha or as Manglik should recount this Chalisa for benefic al results. Positive characteristics of Mars-like quality, mental fortitude, unstoppable soul and vitality are guzzled through reciting the Chalisa.

Those with tribulations of Planets Saturn and Mars should recount the Chalisa for positive results.

What is the Ideal Time to Recite Hanuman Chalisa

It is believed that people who have signifi ant tasks to be accomplished should recite these verses 108 times on the auspicious nights of Tuesday, Thursday, Saturday or on a moola nakshatara. One will have all obstacles removed for a good life and furthermore get the insurance and effortlessness of Hanuman when recited around evening time.

॥ दोहा ॥

श्रीगुरु चरन सरोज रज, निज मनु मुकुरु सुधारि।
बरनउँ रघुबर बिमल जसु, जो दायकु फल चारि॥

Sri Guru Charan Saroj Raj, Nij Mann Mukuru Sudhaari
Barnaun Raghuvar Bimal Jasu, Jo Daayaku Phal Chaari

Having polished the mirror of my heart with the dust of my Guru's lotus feet, I recite the divine fame of the greatest king of Raghukul dynasty, which bestows us with the fruit of all the four efforts.

बुद्धिहीन तनु जानके, सुमिरौं पवन-कुमार।
बल बुधि बिद्या देहु मोहिं, हरहु कलेस बिकार ॥

Buddhiheen Tanu Janike, Sumiraun Pawan-Kumar
Bal Buddhi Vidya Dehu Mohi, Harahu Kalesh Bikaar

Knowing that this mind of mine has less intelligence, I remember the 'Son of Wind' who, granting me strength, wisdom, and all kinds of knowledge, removes all my suffering and shortcomings.

॥ चौपाई ॥

जय हनुमान ज्ञान गुन सागर ।
जय कपीस तिहुँ लोक उजागर ॥

Jai Hanuman Gyan Gunn Sagar
Jai Kapees Tihun Lok Ujaagar

Victory to Lord Hanuman, the ocean of wisdom and virtue.
Victory to the Lord who is supreme among the monkeys, illuminator of the three worlds.

राम दूत अतुलित बल धामा।
अंजनि पुत्र पवनसुत नामा॥

Ramdoot Atulit Baldhama
Anjani-Putra Pawansut Naama

You are Lord Rama's emissary, the abode of matchless power, Mother Anjani's son, and also popular as the 'Son of the Wind'.

महाबीर बिक्रम बजरंगी।
कुमति निवार सुमति के संगी॥

Mahaveer Vikram Bajrangi
Kumati Nivaar Sumati Ke Sangi

Great hero, You are as mighty as a thunderbolt. You remove evil intellect and are the companion of those having good ones.

कंचन बरन बिराज सुबेसा।
कानन कुण्डल कुँचित केसा ॥४

Kanchan Baran Biraj Subesa
Kaanan Kundal Kunchit Kesa

Your skin is golden in color and You are adorned with beautiful clothes.
You have adorning earrings in Your ears and Your hair is curly and thick.

हाथ बज्र अरु ध्वजा बिराजै ।
काँधे मूँज जनेउ साजै ॥

Haath Braj Au Dhwaja Biraaje
Kaandhe Moonj Janeu Saaje

In Your hands, shine a mace and a flag of righteousness.
A sacred thread adorns Your right shoulder.

शंकर स्वयं/सुवन केसरी नंदन।
तेज प्रताप महा जगवंदन॥

Shankar Suvan Kesarinandan
Tej Prataap Maha Jag Bandan

You are the embodiment of Lord Shiva and vanar-raj Kesari's son.
There is no limit or end to Your glory, Your magnificence.
The whole Universe worships You.

बिद्यावान गुनी अति चातुर।
राम काज करिबे को आतुर॥

Vidyavaan Guni Ati Chaatur
Ram Kaaj Karibe Ko Aatur

You are the wisest of the wise, virtuous and (morally) clever.
You are always eager to do Lord Rama's works.

प्रभु चरित्र सुनिबे को रसिया।
राम लखन सीता मन बसिया ॥८

Prabhu Charitra Sunibe Ko Rasiya
Ram Lakhan Sita Mann Basiya

You feel extremely delighted in listening to Lord Rama's doings and conduct.
Lord Rama, Mother Sita, and Lord Laxmana dwell forever in Your heart.

सूक्ष्म रूप धरि सियहिं दिखावा।
बिकट रूप धरि लंक जरावा ॥

Sukshma Roop Dhari Siyanhi Dikhawa
Bikat Roop Dhari Lanka Jarawa

Taking the subtle form, You appeared in front of Mother Sita.
And, taking the formidable form, You burnt the Lanka (Ravana's kingdom).

भीम रूप धरि असुर सँहारे।
रामचन्द्र के काज सँवारे॥

Bheem Roop Dhari Asura Sanghare
Ramchandra Ke Kaaj Sanware

Taking the massive form (like that of Bheema), You slaughtered the demons. This is how, You completed Lord Rama's tasks, successfully.

लाय सजीवन लखन जियाए।
श्री रघुबीर हरषि उर लाये ॥

Laaye Sanjeevan Lakhana Jiyaaye
Sri Raghuveer Harashi Urr Laaye

Bringing the magic-herb (sanjivani), You revived Lord Laxmana.

रघुपति कीन्ही बहुत बड़ाई।
तुम मम प्रिय भरतहि सम भाई ॥१२

Raghupati Keenhi Bahut Badai
Tum Mum Priya, Bhartahi Sum Bhai

Raghupati, Lord Rama praised You greatly and overflowing in gratitude, said that You are a dear brother to Him just as Bharat is.

सहस बदन तुम्हरो जस गावैं।
अस कहि श्रीपति कण्ठ लगावैं॥

Sahas Badan Tumharo Jas Gaave
Asa Kahi Sripati Kanth Lagaave

Saying this, Lord Rama drew You to Himself and embraced you.
Sages like Sanaka, Gods like Brahma and sages like Narada and even the thousand-mouthed serpent sing Your fame!

सनकादिक ब्रह्मादि मुनीसा।
नारद सारद सहित अहीसा॥

Sankaadik Brahmadi Munisa
Narad Sarad Sahit Aheesa

Sanak, Sanandan and the other Rishis and great saints; Brahma - the god, Narada, Saraswati - the Mother Divine and the King of serpents sing Your glory.

जम कुबेर दिगपाल जहाँ ते।
कबि कोबिद कहि सके कहाँ ते ॥

Jam Kuber Digpal Jahan Te
Kabi Kobid Kahi Sake Kahan Te

Yama, Kubera and the guardians of the four quarters; poets and scholars - none can express Your glory.

तुम उपकार सुग्रीवहिं कीह्ना।
राम मिलाय राज पद दीह्ना ॥१६

Tum Upkaar Sugreevahi Keenha
Ram Milaaye Raj-Pad Deenha

You helped Sugriva by introducing Him to Lord Rama and regaining his crown.
Therefore, You gave Him the Kingship (the dignity of being called a king).

तुम्हरो मंत्र बिभीषण माना ।
लंकेश्वर भए सब जग जाना ॥

Tumharo Mantra Bibhishan Maana
Lankeshwar Bhaye Sab Jag Jaana

Likewise, complying with Your preachings, even Vibhishana became the King of Lanka.

जुग सहस्त्र जोजन पर भानु ।
लील्यो ताहि मधुर फल जानू ॥

Yug Sahastra Jojan Par Bhanu
Leelyo Taahi Madhur Phal Jaanu

You swallowed the sun, located thousands of miles away, mistaking it as a sweet, red fruit!

प्रभु मुद्रिका मेलि मुख माहीं।
जलधि लाँघि गये अचरज नाहीं॥

Prabhu Mudrika Meli Mukh Maahi
Jaladhi Laandhi Gaye Achraj Naahi

Keeping the ring in Your mouth, which was given to You by Lord Rama, you crossed over the Ocean, to no astonishment, whatsoever.

दुर्गम काज जगत के जेते ।
सुगम अनुग्रह तुम्हरे तेते ॥२०

Durgam Kaaj Jagat Ke Jete
Sugam Anugrah Tumhare Tete

All difficult tasks of this world become easy, with Your grace.

राम दुआरे तुम रखवारे ।
होत न आज्ञा बिनु पैसारे ॥

Ram Duaare Tum Rakhvare
Hott Na Aagya Binu Paisare

You are the guardian at Lord Rama's door. Nobody can move forward without Your permission which means that Lord Rama's darshans (to get the sight of) are possible only with Your blessings.

सब सुख लहै तुम्हारी सरना।
तुम रक्षक काहू को डरना॥

Sab Sukh Lahe Tumhari Sarna
Tum Rakshak Kahu Ko Dar Na

Those who take refuge in You, find all the comforts and happiness.
When we have a protector like You, we do not need to get scared of anybody or anything.

आपन तेज सम्हारो आपै ।
तीनों लोक हाँक तै काँपै ॥

Aapan Tej Samharo Aape
Teeno Lok Haank Te Kaanpe

You alone can withstand Your magnificence. All the three worlds start trembling at one roar of Yours.

भूत पिशाच निकट नहिं आवै।
महावीर जब नाम सुनावै ॥२४

Bhoot Pishaach Nikat Nahi Aavein
Mahaveer Jab Naam Sunaave

O Mahaveer! No ghosts or evil spirits come near the ones who remember Your name. Therefore, just remembering Your name does everything!

नासै रोग हरै सब पीरा ।
जपत निरंतर हनुमत बीरा ॥

Naase Rog Hare Sab Peera
Japat Nirantar Hanumat Beera

O Hanuman! All diseases and all kinds of pain get eradicated when one recites or chants Your name. Therefore, chanting Your name regularly is considered to be very significant.

संकट तै हनुमान छुडावै।
मन क्रम बचन ध्यान जो लावै॥

Sankat Te Hanuman Churave
Mann Kram Vachan Dhyaan Jo Laave

Whoever meditates upon or worships You with thought, word, and deed, gets freedom from all kinds of crisis and affliction.

सब पर राम तपस्वी राजा।
तिनके काज सकल तुम साजा॥

Sab Par Ram Tapasvi Raja
Tin Ke Kaaj Sakal Tum Saaja

Lord Rama is the greatest Ascetic amongst all the Kings.
But, it's only You who carried out all the tasks of Lord Sri Rama.

और मनोरथ जो कोई लावै ।
सोई अमित जीवन फल पावै ॥२८

Aur Manorath Jo Koi Laave
Soi Amit Jivan Phal Paave

One who comes to You with any longing or a sincere desire obtains the abundance of the manifested fruit, which remains undying throughout life.

चारों जुग परताप तुम्हारा।
है परसिद्ध जगत उजियारा॥

Chaaron Yug Partap Tumhara
Hai Parsidh Jagat Ujiyara

Your splendor fills all the Four Ages.
And, Your glory is renowned throughout the world.

साधु सन्त के तुम रखवारे ।
असुर निकंदन राम दुलारे ॥

Saadhu-Sant Ke Tum Rakhvare
Asur Nikandan Ram Dulaare

You are the guardian of saints and sages; the destroyer of demons and adored by Lord Rama.

अष्ट सिद्धि नौ निधि के दाता।
अस बर दीन जानकी माता॥

Ashta Siddhi Nau Nidhi Ke Daata
As Var Deen Janaki Mata

You have been blessed by Mother Janaki to give boon further, to the deserving ones, wherein You can grant the siddhis (eight different powers) and the nidhis (nine different kinds of wealth).

राम रसायन तुम्हरे पासा ।
सदा रहो रघुपति के दासा ॥३२

Ram Rasayan Tumhare Paasa
Sadaa Raho Raghupati Ke Daasa

You have the essence of Ram bhakti, may you always remain the humble and devoted servant of Raghupati.

तुम्हरे भजन राम को पावै।
जनम जनम के दुख बिसरावै ॥

Tumhare Bhajan Ram Ko Paave
Janam Janam Ke Dukh Bisraave

When one sings Your praise, Your name, He gets to meet Lord Rama and finds relief from the sorrows of many lifetimes.

अंतकाल रघुवरपुर जाई।
जहाँ जन्म हरिभक्त कहाई॥

Antkaal Raghuvar Pur Jaayi
Jahan Janam Hari-Bhakt Kahayi

By your grace, one will go to the immortal abode of Lord Rama after death and remain devoted to Him.

और देवता चित्त ना धरई।
हनुमत सेइ सर्ब सुख करई॥

Aur Devta Chitta Na Dharai
Hanumat Sei Sarva Sukh Karai

It is not needed to serve any other Deity or God.
Service to Lord Hanuman gives all the comforts.

संकट कटै मिटै सब पीरा।
जो सुमिरै हनुमत बलबीरा ॥३६

Sankat Kate, Mite Sab Peera
Jo Sumire Hanumat Balbeera

All troubles cease for the one who remembers the powerful lord, Lord Hanuman and all his pains also come to an end.

जै जै जै हनुमान गोसाईं।
कृपा करहु गुरुदेव की नाईं॥

Jai Jai Jai Hanuman Gosain
Krupa Karahu Gurudev Ki Naai

O Lord Hanuman! Praises and glory to you O mighty Lord, please bestow your grace as our Supreme Guru.

जो सत बार पाठ कर कोई ।
छूटहि बंदि महा सुख होई ॥

Jo Sat Baar Paath Kar Koi
Chutahi Bandhi Maha Sukh Hoyi

One who recites this Chalisa a hundred times is released from all bondages and will attain great bliss.

जो यह पढ़ै हनुमान चालीसा ।
होय सिद्धि साखी गौरीसा ॥

Jo Yeh Padhe Hanuman Chalisa
Hoye Siddhi Saakhi Gaurisa

One who reads and recites this Hanuman Chalisa,
all his works get accomplished.
Lord Shiva, Himself, is the witness to it.

तुलसीदास सदा हरि चेरा।
कीजै नाथ हृदय मह डेरा ॥४०

Tulsidas Sada Hari Chera
Keeje Nath Hriday Mah Dera

O Lord Hanuman, May I always remain a servant, a devotee to Lord Sri Ram, says Tulsidas. And, May You always reside in my heart.

॥ दोहा ॥

पवन तनय संकट हरन, मंगल मूरति रूप।
राम लखन सीता सहित, हृदय बसहु सुर भूप॥

Pawan Tanay Sankat Haran, Mangal Murti Roop
Ram Lakhan Sita Sahit, Hriday Basahu Sur Bhoop

O the Son of Wind, You are the destroyer of all sorrows.
You are the embodiment of fortune and prosperity.
With Lord Rama, Laxmana and Mother Sita, dwell in my heart, always.

Birth and Childhood of Hanuman

Hanuman's lineage is shrouded in fascinating mythological tales. He was born to Kesari, a vanar, and was the grandson of King Brihaspati of Sumeru. Hanuman's mother, Anjana, originally an apsara from the celestial realms, descended to the mortal world due to a curse. Anjana and Kesari embarked on a 12-year period of rigorous penance and prayer, ultimately receiving a divine boon from Lord Shiva, who granted them a child. That child was none other than Hanuman, often regarded as a refl ction or embodiment of Lord Shiva himself. It's worth noting that some myths also depict Hanuman as the son of the Wind God, Vayu Dev, based on the popular story of Vayu Dev delivering sacred pudding to Anjana, stemming from King Dasharatha's Putrakama Yagya ritual. Th s pudding was consumed by King Dasharatha's three wives, leading to the birth of Rama, Lakshmana, Bharata, and Shatrughna. During her prayers to Shiva, the god channeled Vayu Dev's energy into Anjana's womb, giving rise to the association of Hanuman as Vayuputra.

Hanuman's early adventures have been a source of captivating tales passed down through generations. As a restless and adventurous child, Hanuman once mistook the sun for a ripe mango and chased it with the intention of consuming it. During this pursuit, he encountered Rahu, a Vedic planet also pursuing the sun for an eclipse. Hanuman valiantly thwarted Rahu's efforts to reach the sun fi st, which incurred the wrath of Lord Indra. In response, Indra struck Hanuman with a thunderbolt, causing him to plummet to Earth, unconscious, and leaving a permanent mark on his chin. Vayu Dev, Hanuman's father figu e, was furious and withdrew all the air from the universe. Witnessing the suffering of all living beings, Lord Indra revoked the effect of the thunderbolt, revived Hanuman, and granted him numerous boons, with the blessings of the devas, to appease Vayu Dev.

These boons included an irrevocable curse from Brahma, ensuring Hanuman's invulnerability to any weapon in battle. Shiva bestowed him with longevity, scriptural wisdom, the ability to traverse the ocean, and a protective band. Varuna blessed him with immunity from water, Agni Dev protected him from fi e, and Surya Dev granted him the powers of "laghima" and "garima," enabling him to assume the smallest or largest form at will. Yama, the God of Death, granted him health and immunity from weapons, rendering him immune to death. Kubera, the treasurer of the Gods, blessed him with eternal happiness and contentment, while Kamadeva, the God of love, declared him a celibate, freeing him from lust. Additionally, his father, Vayu Dev, enhanced his speed. Hanuman later became a student of Surya, acquiring profound knowledge. When he sought to repay his guru dakshina (a token of gratitude to his teacher), Surya directed him to assist Sugriva, Surya's spiritual son, leading to Hanuman's pivotal role as Sugriva's minister.

What does 'Hanuman' mean?

The name "Hanuman" holds two distinct interpretations. In the fi st, "Hanu" signifies "jaw," and "Man(t)" denotes "disfigu ed." According to mythology, Lord Indra disfigu ed Hanuman's jaw when he mistook the sun for a fruit and attempted to consume it.

The second interpretation derives from "Han," signifying "killed" or "destroyed," and "Man," representing "pride." Both interpretations converge on the concept of one who has vanquished their pride. Hanuman embodies humility, lacking arrogance or ego, which are fundamental attributes for achieving success in life. While we may rightfully take pride in our accomplishments, it is imperative never to exhibit arrogance or conceit.

Hanuman – Parents and Guru

According to legend, Anjana, a beautiful Apsara in Lord Brahma's celestial court, fell under the curse of a sage. The curse dictated that her face would transform into that of a monkey the moment she fell in love. Lord Brahma, in his benevolence, offered her a blessing: once she bore a son, the curse would be lifted, and she would return to Brahmalok. Anjana took human birth on Earth and eventually fell in love with Kesari, the monkey king, leading to their marriage. Her unwavering devotion to Lord Shiva continued as she sought to please the deity. Impressed by her dedication, Lord Shiva granted her wish to be his mother, thereby relieving her of the sage's curse.

In due course, King Dasarath conducted a yagna, during which a sage provided him with kheer to feed his wives. A kite seized a portion of this kheer, carrying it to Anjana, who was in meditation. Lord Vayu (Pawan - Wind), under Lord Shiva's direction, placed the kheer in Anjana's hand. Believing it to be Lord Shiva's prasad, she consumed it, giving rise to the birth of Hanuman, the incarnation of the Lord of the Winds.

This narrative establishes Lord Hanuman as an avatar of Lord Shiva and the son of Kesari and Anjana, as well as Lord Vayu. Kesari, denoting "Lion," symbolizes courage, while Anjana embodies "pure intelligence" and "divine grace." Vayu represents qualities like strength, speed, and purity. The analogy drawn here is that just as one opens a closed room to allow fresh air in for purification, success in life necessitates both strength and purity. While a strong individual may not always possess purity, a pure individual inherently possesses strength. Hanuman epitomizes this dual quality of strength and purity.

Lord Surya served as Hanuman's Guru. When Hanuman approached Lord Surya to be his teacher, he initially declined, citing his busy schedule. However, he agreed to mentor Hanuman under the condition that Hanuman could match his pace while walking backward during lessons. Hanuman accepted the challenge and rapidly acquired knowledge of the Vedas and shastras.

Becoming a respected scholar demands unwavering commitment, hard work, and the ability to surmount obstacles. Hanuman serves as an emblem of these qualities, signifying that one can aspire to become like him by emulating his characteristics.

Surya and Vayu, representing Guru and Father, exemplify selflessness and purity. Surya provides light and warmth to all, regardless of their nature, mirroring Vayu's life-giving essence. Both entities serve as purifiers. Notably, Vayu serves selflessly without drawing attention to its presence, emphasizing the importance of rendering unconditional service to humanity. By serving society in the selfless manner of Surya and Vayu, one can attain significant success in life

Hanuman's Attributes

Hanuman has several attributes or qualities that make him a model whose example Hindus can follow. These attributes represent some of the core concepts of Hinduism - here's some of them:

Tantra means 'weaving'. Hanuman is connected to the Hindu belief that all living things are connected, or 'woven together'.

Brahmachari means 'self-control'. Hindus need to be able to control their desires for things like money and pleasure, so that they can focus on more important things like helping others.

The Hindu concepts of Kurūp and Sundar mean that while someone can be 'ugly on the outside' (Kurūp), if they are a good Hindu they will be 'beautiful on the inside' (Sundar).

Kama-rupin means 'shapeshifting', meaning that Hanuman can become smaller than the smallest opening or larger than the largest opponent. Th s is connected to the Hindu concept of Vighnahartā, which means 'removing obstacles'. Hindus believe that the Gods and Goddesses can help them overcome any problem.

Hinduism encourages a combination of the values of Shakti and Bhakti. Shakti means 'strength' or 'power', while Bhakti is 'devotion' or 'worship'. A good Hindu should be strong and powerful, but should use their power in devotion to the Gods and to help other people, rather than for their own interest.

Reaching for the Sun

One morning when he was a young child, Hanuman woke up and felt extremely hungry. He saw a big sphere fl ating above him, bright red and glistening. Thi king with his belly, Hanuman assumed the sphere was a ripe and juicy piece of fruit, so he leapt up to grab and eat it. However, the red sphere was not a piece of fruit, but the rising sun coming up over the horizon!

To punish Hanuman for his mistake and to stop him from snatching the sun out of the sky, the King of Gods Indra intervened and struck Hanuman with a thunderbolt. It hit Hanuman on his chin, and he fell to the earth - dead - and with a broken jaw. Th s is in fact where

Hanuman gets his name: the word Hanuman originally meant 'disfigu ed jaw'.
His father, Vayu the God of air, became very upset and ran away from the world. Th s meant that there was no air for living beings to breathe, so all the gods, people and animals began to suffer terribly. Th s led Lord Shiva, one of the most powerful Gods, to bring Hanuman back to life. Vayu was so relieved that he returned to the world and living beings were able to breathe the air again.

Hanuman Chalisa's Hidden Astronomical Knowledge

In one of the verses of the Hanuman Chalisa, it says, 'Juga Sahastra Yojana Par Bhanu, Leelyo Taahi Madhur Phal Jaanu.' Th s verse translates to: Hanuman has travelled a far distance, such as yuga x sahasra x yojana to meet Bhanu, thinking it to be a sweet fruit.

So, the verse is verse is saying that the sun is yuga (12,000) x sahasra (1000) x yojana (8), that is 96 million miles away from the Earth.

Now, according to the modern Astronomy, the distance between the sun and the Earth is about 93 milllion miles. Th s is very close to the distance mentioned in the Hanuman Chalisa.

Panchamukhi Hanuman

During another pivotal episode within the epic war, Rama and Lakshmana found themselves in the clutches of Mahiravana, a rakshasa and the brother of Ravana. Th s malevolent entity held them captive within his opulent palace located in Patala, the netherworld, intending to offer them as sacrifices o his deity.

In a valiant effort to locate and rescue them, Hanuman embarked on a perilous journey to Patala. Upon his arrival, Hanuman uncovered the daunting challenge that lay ahead: to defeat Mahiravana, he had to extinguish five separate lamps burning in different directions. To overcome this obstacle, Hanuman assumed the form of Panchamukhi, characterized by five distinct faces. Each face represented a divine entity: Sri Varaha facing north, Sri Narasimha facing south, Sri Garuda facing west, Sri Hayagriva facing the sky, and his own face facing the east. By strategically extinguishing the five lamps in unison, Hanuman triumphed over the dark forces and successfully rescued Rama and Lakshmana from the clutches of Mahiravana.

What is the Siginificance of the Five Faces of Panchmukhi Hanuman?

Sri Hanuman (Original) - Facing East

Th s countenance cleanses the soul of all singl imprefections, fostering a pure and untainted mindset. Achiecing success in life necessitates upholding priciples of ethics, integrity, and trust.

Narasimha - Facing South

This aspect banishes the fear instilled by adversaries and bestows the strength to secure victory. Success is often attainable when one possesses the courage to confront challenges head-on.

Garuda - Facing West

Garuda dispels malevolent forces, negating the influence of black magic and negative entities while purging the body of poisonous effects. As Lord Vishnu's divine mount and the sovereign of birds, Garuda represents mental, spiritual, and physical potency.

Varaha - Facing North

Varaha shields against the adverse effects caused by planetary alignments and ushers in prosperity in all its eight forms (Ashta Aishwarya). Progressing in one's career often requires the removal of negative influences and the cultivation of a more favorable image and broader exposure.

Hayagriva - Facing Upward

This visage imparts knowledge, facilitates victory, bestows a harmonious spouse, and blesses with offspring. Success in life is ofte contingent on acquiring the requisite knowledge and skills, as well as receiving support and understanding from one's spouse and children.

Pride and Emotional Attachment of Lord Hanuman

Shortly after being crowned Emperor upon his triumphant return to Ayodhya, Rama undertakes a ceremonial gesture to express gratitude to all his well-wishers. During a grand court ceremony, Rama's friends and allies take turns receiving honors at his throne. In a touching moment, Hanuman approaches without harboring any desire for a reward. Witnessing Hanuman's presence, Rama is overwhelmed with emotion and warmly embraces him. Rama acknowledges that he could never adequately repay or honor Hanuman for the invaluable assistance and unwavering service he received from the noble Vanara.

Sita, Rama's devoted wife, insists that Hanuman is the most deserving of honor among all. She gifts him a ecklace adorned with precious gemstones from her own neck. Upon receiving the necklace, Hanuman immediately dismantles it and examines each stone closely. Th s action perplexes many in attendance, prompting them to inquire why he is dismantling such a precious gift

Hanuman's response is profound. He explains that he was inspecting the stones to ensure that Rama and Sita were within them because, without their presence, the necklace held no value to him. In a remarkable display of devotion, Hanuman, to the astonishment of all, tears open his chest, revealing the divine images of Rama and Sita literally residing within his heart.

Th s poignant incident serves as a poignant testament to the boundless love, dedication, and loyalty that Hanuman held for Sita and Rama. It exemplifies he kind of unwavering commitment and loyalty that is essential for individuals within an organization to achieve great success. It's akin to patriotism, where one is willing to go the extra mile for the organization's success, knowing that their dedication and loyalty will ultimately be richly rewarded.

Hanuman and Yoga

If yoga is defi ed as the art of mastering one's mind, then Hanuman epitomizes the quintessential yogi, possessing flawless control over his senses. He attains this mastery through a disciplined way of life, guided by the twin pillars of celibacy and selfle s devotion (bhakti). Hanuman stands as the ultimate exemplar of a Brahmachari, dedicated to the path of Brahma. Moreover, he exemplifies he essence of a true karma yogi, carrying out his actions with detachment, functioning as an instrument of destiny rather than being driven by selfish motives.

The Story of Orange Coloured Hanuman

One day, Sita adorned a red powder, sindoor, in the parting of her hair. Hanuman, filled with curiosity, approached her and inquired about the signifi ance of this red powder. Sita explained, "Hanuman, this is sindoor. It brings happiness to Lord Rama and bestows upon him a long and prosperous life."

Upon hearing this, Hanuman vanished from the spot, returning with his entire body, including his clothing, completely covered in red sindoor. When Lord Rama saw Hanuman adorned with sindoor, he inquired about the reason. Hanuman responded, "Sita mata informed me that by applying a small pinch of sindoor on her forehead daily, it would ensure a long and joyful life for you. I pondered, if a mere pinch can have such an effect, what would happen if I covered my entire body with sindoor?"

Consequently, Lord Rama granted a boon to all his devoted followers, decreeing that those who apply sindoor to Hanuman and perform Hanuman puja with sindoor would be blessed with a long and joyful life, with their wishes fulfil ed.

Hanuman, as Rama's Devotee

In Valmiki's fi h book of the Ramayana, titled Sundara Kanda, we fi d a detailed account of Hanuman's encounter with Rama and Lakshamana, along with the subsequent adventures that unfold. Rama and Lakshamana, while traversing the forests of Kishkindha in search of Sita, who had been abducted by Ravana, come across Hanuman and Sugriva. Initially, Sugriva harbors suspicions regarding the identities of Rama and Lakshmana, fearing that they might be spies sent by his brother Vali. Hanuman, however, is more confide t in his assessment, recognizing Rama and Lakshmana as dignifi d warriors. Nevertheless, to be absolutely certain, Sugriva dispatches Hanuman in the guise of a Brahmin to ascertain their true identities and the purpose of their visit.

Upon meeting Hanuman, Rama is greatly impressed by his exceptional manners and impeccable speech. Rama perceives in Hanuman the qualities of a trustworthy friend, someone upon whom he can depend, especially in this time of crisis with Sita's disappearance. When Rama fi ally reveals his true identity to Hanuman, Hanuman discards his disguise and prostrates at Rama's feet, seeking his blessings. Th s marks the commencement of an epic friendship between Rama and his most devoted disciple. Even today, people cite their relationship as an exemplary instance of the fi est friendship in Hindu mythology. Hanuman is often depicted as opening his chest to reveal the images of Rama and Sita, underlining his status as the greatest devotee ever born on Earth.

Subsequently, Hanuman introduces Rama to Sugriva and elaborates on the situation with Sugriva's brother, Vali. Rama assists Sugriva in reclaiming his kingdom from Vali by defeating Vali in combat. In gratitude, Sugriva pledges to provide Rama with an army of vanars to aid in the quest to fi d Sita. These vanars are dispatched in all four directions to scour the Earth for information, ultimately bringing back the news that Sita is held captive in Lanka.

Hanuman's Effort in Finding Sita Devi

Hanuman, propelled by his extraordinary strength, accomplished the incredible feat of leaping across the ocean to reach Lanka from the Indian mainland. As he gazed upon Lanka from his vantage point, he couldn't help but be captivated by its resplendent beauty and opulence.

In the heart of Lanka's Ashoka groves, Hanuman discovered Sita held in captivity. Filled with deep concern and a genuine desire to reunite her with Rama, Hanuman implored Sita to accompany him back to her beloved husband. He assured her of the relentless efforts he had exerted in search of her. However, Sita, steadfast in her devotion and integrity, declined Hanuman's plea, explaining that returning with him alone would be a dishonor to Rama. She insisted that she would only return with Rama himself. Before parting, Hanuman cntrusted Sita with a ring from Rama as a token of their enduring love.

Following his encounter with Sita, Lanka was thrown into chaos as Hanuman unleashed havoc upon the city. Single-handedly, he laid waste to palaces and properties, vanquishing many rakshasas, including Jambumali and Aksha Kumar. Hanuman even staged a ruse of being captured by Ravana's son, Indrajit, in order to confront Ravana himself.

In his audience with Ravana, Hanuman delivered an ultimatum, urging the demon king to release Sita and warning that he would be forgiven if he did so honorably. Th s proposition greatly infuriated Ravana, leading to the cruel order to set Hanuman's tail ablaze. Hanuman, allowing his tail to burn for a moment, leaped from rooftop to rooftop, setting large portions of Lanka ablaze and eluding his captors. Eventually, he made a daring escape and returned to Rama by leaping over the ocean, landing safely back in India.

Hanuman Lifting Dronagiri Mountain to Bring Sanjivani

Lakshmana had sustained grave injuries during his fie ce battle against Ravana's son, Indrajit. In a bid to restore Lakshmana's health, Rama entrusted Hanuman with the vital mission of procuring a potent life-restoring herb called Sanjivani from the Dronagiri Mountains in the Himalayas.

Ravana, upon learning of this mission, hatched a malevolent plan to ensure Lakshmana's demise, understanding that Rama would be overwhelmed with grief and unable to continue the war. He dispatched the sinister witch Kalanemi to obstruct Hanuman's quest for the herb. Kalanemi, disguised as a sage, initially managed to deceive Hanuman. However, with the assistance of an apsara whom he had liberated from her cursed state as a crocodile, Hanuman unveiled Kalanemi's true identity and ultimately defeated her.

Undeterred, Ravana persisted in his efforts and invoked Surya, the Sun God, to rise ahead of schedule. Ravana was well aware that Lakshmana's life hung in the balance, and if he remained untreated until daybreak, his wounds would prove fatal. Recognizing this imminent danger, Hanuman took drastic measures. He expanded his form to many times his usual size, effectively obstructing the appearance of the Sun God.

As Hanuman continued his search for the precious herb, he encountered a dilemma. He struggled to identify the specific erb required to heal Lakshmana. In a remarkable display of strength, Hanuman resolved this issue by uprooting and carrying the entire mountain, owing to his limitless might. He transported the mountain to the battlefi ld in Lanka, where Sushena, the physician, was able to discern the herb needed to revive Lakshmana successfully.

Overwhelmed with gratitude, Rama warmly embraced Hanuman for his extraordinary efforts in saving his beloved brother. Hanuman then released Surya from his powerful grip and sought forgiveness, as Surya had been his revered teacher.

Why Images of Hanuman Ji are Used on Amulets and Jewelry

As the relentless battle with Ravana unfolded, the demon king suffered grievous losses, with his brothers and sons falling one by one. It became increasingly evident that Ravana was on the path to inevitable defeat. In a desperate bid, Ravana summoned his only surviving son, Mahiravana, a formidable sorcerer who held dominion over the underworld, known as Patala Loka. Mahiravana was a devout worshiper of Goddess Kali, from whom he had acquired potent occult knowledge. Initially, Mahiravana was reluctant to join the confli t against Rama, recognizing the righteousness of Rama's cause. However, understanding Mahiravana's vulnerability to ritual magic, Ravana cunningly appealed to his weaknesses.

Ravana enticed Mahiravana by suggesting, "Consider the extraordinary powers that Goddess Kali will bestow upon you when you offer her the heads of two handsome and virile youths like Rama and Lakshmana." It was not surprising that Mahiravana succumbed to this temptation.

The malevolent sorcerer, Mahiravana, devised a scheme to kidnap both Rama and his brother Lakshmana while they were in slumber. In their place, he left a ark trail leading deep into the depths of the earth. Swiftly, Hanuman embarked on a courageous journey, diving into the tunnel and venturing into Patala, the subterranean realm ruled by Mahiravana. There, he discovered the two brothers bound to a post, their bodies anointed with mustard oil and adorned with marigold fl wers, awaiting a gruesome sacrific . Nearby, Mahiravana was honing the sacrific al blade and reciting invocations to invoke the goddess.

With cunning strategy, Hanuman transformed into a bee and whispered into Rama's ear, "When Mahiravana instructs you to place your neck on the sacrific al block, inform him that, due to your royal lineage, you have never learned to bow your head. Request him to demonstrate the proper way to perform such an act." Mahiravana fell into the trap, bowing his head according to the prescribed ritual. In that moment, Hanuman revealed his true form, swiftly seized the blade, and beheaded the sorcerer. Thus, Hanuman skillfully reversed the situation, offering Mahiravana as a sacrifice o Mother Goddess Kali. Impressed by his devotion and valor, Goddess Kali appointed Hanuman as her guardian, leading to the tradition of monkey deities guarding the entrances of many temples dedicated to her. To this day, Hanuman is invoked for protection against sorcery, and amulets and charms bearing his likeness remain highly sought after by devotees.

Why Hanuman Ji is Shown Tearing Open his Own Chest

Once, Sita bestowed upon Hanuman a necklace adorned with pearls. After some time, the residents of Ayodhya noticed him carefully breaking the necklace and meticulously examining each pearl. Intrigued by his actions, they inquired about the reason behind this behavior. Hanuman, with unwavering devotion, replied, "I am searching for Rama and Sita."

Amused by what they perceived as his innocence, the onlookers pointed out that the royal couple was presently seated on the imperial throne. To this, Hanuman responded with profound wisdom, "But Rama and Sita are omnipresent, residing even within my heart." His profound devotion and understanding surpassed their comprehension.

Undeterred, they continued to jest, saying, "If Rama and Sita indeed reside within your heart, can you reveal them to us?" Without hesitation, Hanuman rose to his feet and, using his sharp talons, gently tore open his chest. To their astonishment, within the pulsating depths of his heart, they beheld an image of Rama and Sita enshrined there.

From that moment on, no one dared to mock or trivialize Hanuman's devotion, for they had witnessed the depth of his unwavering love and commitment to Lord Rama and Sita.

Hanuman's Power - Ashta Siddhis and Nava Nidhis

Lord Hanuman is believed to have got Ashta-Siddhi (eight divine powers) and Nav-Nidhi (nine more powers). Siddha has no eqiuvalent in English language, it can be understood as combinatino of perfection and establishment (when both are used simultaneously, i.e. Perfection+Established or perfectly established).

In hanuman chalisa the siddhi word means that person has attained such qualities by establishing himself into perfect self or atman. In Hinduism, eight siddhis (Ashta Siddhi) or Eight great perfections (mahasiddhi) are described as follows:

1) अणिमा Animā: reducing one's body even to the size of an atom
2) महिमा Mahima: expanding one's body to an infin tely large size
3) गरिमा Garima: becoming infin tely heavy
4) लघिमा Laghima: becoming almost weightless
5) प्राप्ति Prāpti: having unrestricted access to all place

6) प्राकाम्या Prākāmya: realizing whatever one desires

7) ईशत्व Istva: possessing absolute lordship

8) वस्तव Vaśtva: the power to subjugate all

The masters of yoga speak of eighteen mystical perfections [siddhis] and meditations [leading to siddhis]. Eight of them are [primary and] prominent in Me and ten of them [are secondary and] originate from the quality [of goodness].

Nidhi In Sanskrit means treasure there are 9 (primary)types of treasures or valuable possessions.

The nava nidhis are:

1) mahapadma "great lotus fl wer"
2) padma "lotus fl wer"
3) shankha "conch"
4) makara "crocodile"
5) kachchhapa "tortoise"
6) kumud "a particular precious stone"
7) kunda "jasmine"
8) nila "sapphire"
9) kharva "dwarf"

Hanuman's Role in Mahabharata

Hanuman, one of the Chiranjeevis, has been blessed with the ability to live eternally. Lord Hanuman's presence extends beyond the Ramayana, as he is also refereneced in the epic Mahabharata. Notably, Hanuman shares a connection with Bhima, one of the Pandava brothers, through their shared lineage as sons of Vayu, the wind god. Hanuman's signifi ance is highlighted twice in the Mahabharata, underscoring his enduring importance in Hindu mythology.

The fi st mention of Hanuman in the Mahabharata occurs when he encounters Bhima during the period of exile endured by the Pandavas. Hanuman's second signifi ant appearance is during the great battle of Kurukshetra, where he defends Arjuna's chariot by residing on its flag. These pivotal interactions unfold within the broader narrative of the Mahabharata.

In one memorable episode, Hanuman takes on the guise of a common monkey in the sacred city of Rameshwaram. Arjuna, one of the Pandava princes, is awe-struck by the grand bridge that spans to Lanka, which was constructed by Lord Ram and the vanaras (monkeys). He wonders aloud why Lord Ram required the assistance of monkeys and expresses his belief that he could have built such a bridge using his arrows. Hanuman, still appearing as a monkey, cautioningly advises Arjuna that a bridge made of arrows would not withstand the weight of even a single person. Arjuna, considering it a challenge, agrees to construct such a bridge and pledges to end his own life if it collapses.

Arjuna proceeds to use his divine arrows to build a bridge, and Hanuman courageously walks across it, causing it to collapse instantly. Overwhelmed by this failure, Arjuna contemplates taking his own life. However, at that precise moment, Lord Krishna appears and, through His divine power, reconstructs the bridge. He instructs Hanuman to traverse it once more, and this time, it remains stable. Th s transformative event leads Hanuman to reveal his true form and offer his assistance to Arjuna in the impending battle. During the epic battle of Kurukshetra, Lord Hanuman occupies a prominent position on the flag of Arjuna's chariot. On the penultimate day of the war, Lord Krishna advises Arjuna to dismount from the chariot before He does so Himself. Krishna commends Hanuman for his unwavering presence, ensuring the safety of the chariot even after Arjuna's departure. As Hanuman departs from the chariot, it miraculously bursts into flames, leaving Arjuna in profound amazement. Lord Krishna later reveals that without Hanuman's divine protection, the chariot would have succumbed to celestial weaponry.

In conclusion, Lord Hanuman plays a signifi ant role in both the Ramayana and the Mahabharata, showcasing his enduring importance in Hindu mythology and underscoring his unwavering devotion and divine assistance in pivotal moments.

When Bhima met Hanuman

During the era of the Mahabharata, a signifi ant encounter transpired between Bhima and Lord Hanuman. Th s event unfolded when Draupadi, the esteemed wife of the Pandavas, requested Bhima to retrieve the Saugandhika fl wers for her during their exile. Bhima embarked on a quest to fi d these blossoms, but his journey took an unexpected turn.

As Bhima ventured through the forest, he came across a colossal monkey comfortably occupying the path. Frustrated by this obstacle, Bhima demanded that the monkey move aside to allow him to pass. However, the monkey, aged and unable to move on his own, humbly implored Bhima not to force him to move. He explained that his inability to move was the reason for his request, suggesting that Bhima could gently shift h s tail aside and proceed.

In his annoyance, Bhima attempted to use his mighty mace to push the monkey's tail out of the way. Yet, to his astonishment, the tail remained steadfast and unyielding. After an arduous struggle, Bhima gradually comprehended that this was no ordinary monkey. Recognizing his own limitations, Bhima eventually conceded defeat and earnestly sought forgiveness.

It was then that Lord Hanuman revealed his true divine form and bestowed his blessings upon Bhima, recognizing the sincerity of his humility and devotion. Th s remarkable encounter served as a profound lesson in humility and reverence for Bhima, as he came to realize the divine presence and grace that had guided his path.

Temples of Lord Hanuman

Salasar Hanuman Temple, Salasar, Rajasthan

In Churu district of Rajasthan, is a small village called Salasar. In this village, there is a statue of Hanuman which has beard and mustache too. It is believed that this Hanuman statue was found by a farmer while walking around a fi ld. The idol has been placed on a gold throne now.

Hanumandhara, Chitrakut

Near Chitrakut, there is a small place called Hanumandhara. Here there is an old idol of Lord Hanuman standing against a mountain for years. And a small water fl w that meets the river touches this idol.

Mehandipur Balaji Temple, Dausa, Rajasthan

Rajasthan's Dausa district, which is nestled between two mountains is a place called Mehndipur. It has a very large rock in the shape of Hanuman that had recovered itself. It is believed to be Sri Hanuman. There is a small water pond in the idol's feet whose water never gets over.

Hanumangadhi, Ayodhya

The Hanumangadhi temple is in Ayodhya. It is situates on the right side bank of river Saryu on a high hill. People have to climb 76 stairs to reach this temple. The Hanuman idol installed here is only 6 inches long, which is always, adorned with garlands.

Sankatmochan Temple, Varanasi (UP)

Th s is an ancient place associated with Hanuman's name. Here is a huge temple known as Sankatmochan. It is believed that Tulsidas had himself established this temple.

Shri Hanuman Temple, Jamnagar (Gujarat)

In 1540, along with Jamnagar, this temple of Lord Hanuman was also established. Here, since 1964, the rama dhuni is continuously being sung and this is why its name is also mentioned in the guineas book of world records.

Mahavir Hanuman Mandir, Patna (Bihar)

Right opposite Patna junction, there is a famous temple of Lord Hanuman called Mahavir Temple. In Northern India, after the Vaishno Devi Temple, this temple gets the maximum offerings.

Hanuman Temple, Allahabad (UP)

Attached to the Allahabad fort, this temple has the idol of Hanuman which is lying. Th s idol of Hamuman is 20 feet long.

Shri Panchmukh Aanjanayar Swami Ji, Kumbakonam (Tamil Nadu)

The idol at the Panchmukh Aanjanayar swami temple is in the form of Panchmukhi Hanuman.

Hanuman Mantra

A person who regularly recites the Hanuman mantra is never troubled by Ghosts, devils or spirits. Hanuman mantra infuses a person with unlimited energy and courage.

Rosary to be used for: Lal chandan ki mala, Lal munga ki mala
Flowers to be used: Lal vastra, Lal aasan, Lal phal, Lal phool
Total Number of Recitaion: 11,000 or 21,000 or 31,000 times
Best Time: Amrit Sidhhi Yog Sidh Muhurt

Lord Hanuman is considered as an embodiment of Lord Shiva and Lord Vishnu. Lord Hanuman is very simple and compassionate; yet he is also very powerful and courageous. Lord Hanuman represents Consciousness or life energy and makes one brave and fearless.

Regular recitation of the Hanuman mantra helps a person to emerge more victorious in his tasks. Hanuman Mantra helps to quickly solve the problems of life such as problems in married life, debt problems, mental disturbances and agony, etc. By chanting the Hanuman Mantra daily, one becomes active and energetic and doesn't experience laziness in doing any work.

Collection of Hanuman Mantra

Hanuman Mantra – 1

Recite this Hanuman Mantra for getting physical strength, stamina and power.

ॐ हनुमते नमः ।

Om Hanumate Namah |

Hanuman Mantra – 2

हं पवन ननदनाय स्वाहा |

Hang Pawan Nandnaay Swaahaa |

Hanuman Mantra – 3

This Hanuman Mantra is a very secret mantra with unlimited power in it. This Hanuman mantra brings instant results. One becomes exceptionally powerful by chanting this hanuman mantra.

हं हनुमते रुद्रात्मकाय हुं फट् |

Hang Hanumate Rudraatmakaay Hung Phatt |

Hanuman Mantra – 4

Recite this Hanuman Mantra 21000 times to eradicate diseases, evil spirits and other types of disturbances in life.

ॐ नमो भगवते आंजनेयाय महाबलाय स्वाहा |

Om Namo Bhagvate Aanjaneyaay Mahaabalaay Swaahaa |

Hanuman Mantra – 5

ॐ ऐं ह्रीं हनुमते रामदूताय लंकाविध्वंसनाय अंजनी गर्भ संभूताय शाकिनी डाकिनी डाकिनी विध्वंसनाय किलिकिलि बुबुकारेण विभिषणाय हनुमद्देवाय ॐ ह्रीं श्रीं हौं हाँ फट् स्वाहा।।

Om Aing Hring Hanumate Ramdutay Lankavidhvansnay Anjani Garbh Sambhutay Shakini Dakini Dakini Vidhvanssnay Kilikili Bubukaren Vibhishanay Hanumaddevay Om Hring Shring Haung Ha Phat Swaha ||

Atmonnati Rudra Gayatri Mantra

ॐ तत्पुरुषाय विद्महे, महादेवाय धीमहि तन्नो रुद्रः प्रचोदयात् ॥

Om Tatpurushaay Vidmahe, Mahadevay Dheemahi Tanno Rudrah Prachodayat ||

Rudra Mantra

ॐ अघोरेभ्योऽथ घोरेभ्यो घोर घोरतरेभ्य:।
सर्वेभ्य: सर्व सर्वेभ्यो नमस्ते अस्तु रूद्र रुपेभ्य:।।
ॐ नमो भगवते रुद्राय ।।

Om Aghorebhyoath Ghorebhyo Ghor
Ghoratebhyah |
Sarvebhyah Sarv Sarvebhyo Namaste Astu
Rudra Rupebhyah ||

Tvarit Rudra Mantra

॥ ॐ यो रुद्रोऽग्नौ योऽप्सुय ओषधीषु यो रुद्रो विश्वाभुवना-
विवेश तस्मै रुद्राय नमोऽस्तु ॥

|| Om Yo Rudroangau Yoapsuy Oshadhishu Yo Rudro Vishvabhuvana-Vivesh Tasmai Rudray Namoastu ||

Laghu Mrityunjay Mantra

॥ॐ ह्रौं जूं सः ॥

|| Om Hraung Jung Sah ||

Dashakshari Mantra

॥ॐ जूं सः मां पालय-पालय ॥

|| Om Jung Sah Mang Paalay-Paalay ||

Dvadashakshari Mantra

॥ ॐ जूं सः मां पालय-पालय सः जूं ॐ ॥

||Om Jung Sah Mang Paalay-Paalay Sah Jung Om ||

Mahamrityunjay Mantra

ॐ ह्रौं ॐ जूं सः भूर्भुवः स्वः ॐ त्र्यम्बकम् यजामहे
सुगन्धिम् पुष्टिवर्धनम् ।
उर्वारूकमिव बन्धनान् मृत्योर्मुक्षीय मा मृतात् भूर्भुवः स्वरों जूं
सः ह्रौं ॐ ॥

Om Hruang Om Jung Sah Bhurbhuvah Swah
Trayambakam Yajamahe Sugandhim
Pustiwardham |
Urwarukmivbandhanaan Mrityormuksheey
mamritat Bhurbhuvah Swaraung Jung Sah
Hraung Om ||

Significance of Hanuman Mantra

"Ram Raksha Strotam", a Sanskrit Strota, a shield of Ram that has lines devoted to the great Hanuman, saying, "Whoever reads this will be protected by Hanuman." Lord Hanuman is one of the important figures of the Hindu epic The Ramayana and its various versions. He is a Hindu god and an ardent devotee of lord Rama. He plays a very important role throughout the epic. We see his loyalty towards Lord Rama and his brave acts throughout the narrative and come to idolize him. Being an immortal (Chiranjivi), he is mentioned in several other texts including The Mahabharata and some Jain texts. Several texts also imply that he is the incarnation of Lord Shiva.

There are numerous temples of Hanuman built everywhere because it is believed that a great warrior like him protects the surrounding areas from demons, evils, darkness and despair. A lot of prayers, hymns, shlokas and mantras are dedicated to Pawan-putra Hanuman. Some of the significant ones are Hanuman Chalisa, Bajranga Baan, Maruti Strotam, Hanumansahasranam strota, Hanuman Bahuk and so on. All these prayers, hymns and Hanuman mantras are written to not only praise all the good deeds done by Lord Hanuman but also to help us acknowledge his bravery and all other virtues that made him a Hindu lord irrespective of the supernatural elements that he was bestowed with. Take the Hanuman Chalisa – it is a forty lined hymn composed by Goswami Tulsidas in praise of Lord Hanuman. He has written this to inspire the spiritual aspirants to become devotees of Lord Rama, so that they are blessed and protected by Hanuman and also they are helped to spiritually progress. Through these mantras people are reminded of Hanuman's greatness and his terrible fights against the unrighteous. Hanuman is an idol of true devotion and chastity amongst the Hindus.

He is a symbol of devotion of the enlightened individual soul to the supreme soul. The prayers are pleas to Lord Hanuman to help us get rid of the 'bad minds' as he is a true companion of the 'good minds'. The 'bad minds' are the evil thoughts and all the vices that we dwell upon and to prevent this we pray to Hanuman who is said to be a companion of the 'good mind' which being the pure virtues that he is bestowed with. People are said to be able to keep diseases at bay just by chanting his name as he is a symbol of not only physical strength but also the very meaning of the word 'strength' in every possible way. These hymns and mantras of Hanuman glorify the purity of his soul and also makes the people realize how much better it feels to be like him with such pure and innocent virtues. The Hanuman mantras are chanted to remove pain from one's life by seeking help from the greatest protector there has ever been, Hanuman. He is believed to bring happiness in everyone's lives with the help of his never ending positive energy. He is worshipped not because of his immortality but because of the virtues that he possesses that sets him apart from all other immortals.

|| समाप्त ||

Made in the USA
Monee, IL
18 October 2026

66048454R00094